The Father & Son

SWIMMING BOOK

The Father & Son

SWIMMING

BOOK

Illustrations by John Cullen Murphy

A Simple, Sure Way to Teach Any Child to Swim

by *Philip E. Moriarty*

with HOWARD LISS

PELHAM BOOKS

First published in Great Britain by
PELHAM BOOKS LTD
52 Bedford Square
*London, W.C.*1
1971

7207 0504 5

Printed in Great Britain by
Hollen Street Press Ltd at Slough,
and bound by Dorstel Press at Harlow, Essex

Contents

Illustrations

Introduction

To the nonswimmer, swimming is a mystery. To the swimmer, it may still be a mystery, because he is not always aware of what it is that enables him to swim. As long as this mystery exists, swimming is psychological as much as it is physical. Therefore, positive thinking plays an important role in learning this skill.

In most cases when a person learns to swim, his teacher is just another member of the group that frequents the swimming area. It can be an older friend or a contemporary who learned to swim at an earlier age, or it can be a parent. The relationship between nonswimmer and swimming instructor is a friendly one. The beginner does not necessarily bring a classroom attitude to his instruction. Rather it is one of encouragement and demonstration by the swimmer, while the nonswimmer imitates what he has seen or been told.

This fact was brought home to me when my daughter,

who was eight years old at the time, succeeded in teaching three five-year-olds to swim in a small backyard plastic pool. As a safety measure, each of those children wore a tin-can flotation device (which will be described later). Her simple method did not require any scientific approach, such as that of a trained instructor, nor did she delve into the numerous theories of child behavior. Her approach was completely natural.

If this method can produce a happy and reasonably skilled child swimmer, why not put it into practice? In fact, it could be profitably studied and adopted by professional teachers.

It should be noted in all fairness that the children taught by my daughter used the pool daily, just as they rode their tricycles, played with dolls, ate, napped, and watched television daily. A key factor in my daughter's success was "environment," for the pool was there and they used it.

Let us assume that you have had some experience as a teacher. After all, as the parent of the child you did help teach the boy (or girl) to walk, feed himself, wash, and dress, all of which required a degree of muscular coordination. But it is to be expected that you desire a better approach to teaching swimming than you now have. Perhaps, then, this simple approach, used by my daughter, is the answer.

The youngsters whom we shall teach are not unduly fragile. Their minds are strong enough to accept well-directed encouragement and discipline if it is presented to them at their own level of intelligence.

Experience shows that for every child under five years of age who is easy to teach, five others will give the teacher some trouble. The difficulty lies in fear of the unknown. The child really does *not know* what will happen to him when he enters the water.

That is why a flotation device is so effective. When he sees other youngsters stay afloat by this means, he will gain a great deal of confidence. He will understand almost immediately that playing in the water is fun. Before long he will accept the challenge to move faster, perhaps jump into the water, open his eyes under water, chase a ball, and join in other fun activities.

The contents of this book will show you the way. The method is simple. And, best of all, it is fun for the child to participate, and for the parent to teach.

1

Is My Child Ready to Swim?

It is the parents who give the child his first conscious introduction to water. As a father or mother you probably recall the pleasure your child experienced during infancy when he was given his daily bath. Completely submerging the entire body (with the exception of the head) was quite normal from about the age of four weeks. Handled carefully, the youngster is almost certain to enjoy splashing in the water, and the bath becomes a pleasant sensation. Therefore, a child is psychologically ready to swim from the time he learns to walk.

A child of two who has had normal growth and has accomplished most of the normal activities is also physically ready to swim. These activities include walking, crawling, climbing stairs, and climbing onto furniture, all of which require some coordination of the arms and legs.

Teaching the Younger Child

The two-year-old is at an age where he may develop un-justified fears. New surroundings and new faces often cause the child to run for the protection of his parents. Dad or Mom should be the first person to take the child for his first "bath" outside his private tub, and during this initial outing nothing that resembles a lesson should be attempted.

For every young child, the first consideration should be his physical comfort. Controlled conditions are not always possible, but there is a "best" facility and condition, just as there is also a "worst." An indoor pool is the best place to introduce the child to bodies of water larger than his bath-tub. The temperature of the water should be near 80 degrees and the room temperature about 10 degrees higher. The pool should be well lighted. If possible, try to choose a pool in a quiet setting, for loud or sudden noises might make a child nervous or frighten him. The shallow end of the pool should be about three or four feet deep—no higher—and that will enable the parent to stand while he assists the child in play for the first few times in the water.

TRAINING TIPS FOR DAD

Hold the child close to your body to assure him of his safety and give him peace of mind. Often your mere physical presence, the closeness of your body to his, will help to erase the youngster's fears.

Attitude is important, the parent's as well as the child's. Although his first experience should be looked upon as fun, an enjoyable time to be shared by father and son, boisterous activities and loud laughter should nonetheless be avoided. Instead, it should be a simple exercise, one of calm, smiling encouragement. Make this first experience as natural as any other "bath" would be.

Teaching the Older Child

It should be noted that a child of two or three will not have the retention ability of a five- or six-year-old. Unless the younger child participates in water activities almost daily, he will, more than likely, forget most of the skills he had in the water only a few months earlier. While younger children have been taught to swim well in many cases, most experiences have proved that the child aged five learns faster and retains his knowledge better and can be involved in group learning better than younger children.

Initial swimming conditions need not be as controlled for the five-year-old as for the younger child, although, once again, the best facilities are always preferable whenever possible. The important factors to be considered are: proper depth of the swimming area, adequate supervision, good flotation devices, and water temperature (water that is too cold may cause youngsters to be tense and irritable).

If the selected area happens to be a lake or the beach, it is profitable to begin the instruction by simply taking the child's hand and walking into the water with him. Your ultimate destination should be that point or depth where the water comes up to your son's waist. However, along the way, you and the boy should stop, kneel down a few times, perhaps sit in water that is a foot deep, or lie down resting on elbows, so that your heads are out of the water. Your primary aim is to get the boy used to being in water which is deeper than his bath.

Waist-deep water for your son may be only about thigh-high for you. Therefore, when that depth has been reached, you can take the boy into your arms and walk out somewhat deeper. He can move his feet about in the water while you are carrying him, and retain the "feel" of what it is like to splash about, yet feel secure in your arms.

In a swimming pool, the initial approach to water would be somewhat different. Most five- or six-year-olds are about three and a half feet tall, and there is seldom a pool where the shallow end is less than three feet deep. Therefore, at best, the water might come up to your son's chin, and probably even higher than that.

To begin, you slide into the water while the boy sits at the pool's edge, with his feet dangling in the water up to the ankle or calf. Have him kick about in order to get used to the temperature and the feel of the water. Then take the boy in your arms and continue as suggested for lake or beach areas.

Beaches and pools both produce the same end result. The youngster finds that water can be a pleasant place for fun, and he builds a sense of trust in his father, knowing that although his feet cannot touch bottom, there is really nothing to fear.

TRAINING TIPS FOR DAD

All children are impressionable. Parents must be cautious in their conversations and attitudes. A careless word from the parent about a long-remembered "bad experience" during his own first attempts to swim may give rise to unreasonable fears in the boy. Remarks such as, "My older brother threw me into deep water over my head and let me shift for myself," or, "I almost swallowed the whole lake before somebody pulled me out," or, "I almost drowned," should be avoided. Put yourself in your son's position; how would *you* feel if you heard an older person—especially your teacher—say such things?

Point out to the boy the pleasures to be gained from knowing how to swim. He can accompany you on fishing trips, on sailing excursions, to a "For Men Only" afternoon of recreation.

But if your son, for any reason, develops a strong apprehension toward learning to swim, postpone the lessons to a later date. It may take more time for him to become accustomed to the water. No two children are alike, any more than any two adults, and simply because some other child is willing to start earlier is no indication that your son will never overcome his fears. It is important to let him proceed at his own pace. However, it will help if he watches other children, at or near his age, who have become proficient enough to play in the water and swim to a degree. He will see them enjoying themselves. And he may soon learn for himself that all his fears are only imaginary.

During the initial training period, there is the possibility that your son may accidentally swallow some water. He may become flustered and upset. Calm him; reassure him; tell him that these things sometimes happen to expert swimmers and the discomfort is only temporary.

B

THE FLOTATION DEVICE

In our approach to teaching a child to swim, we shall use the technique of the dog paddle (or human stroke) supplemented by a flotation device. Perhaps some parents may question the use of what might appear to be a crutch, which will be discarded later. Rest assured that there are valid reasons for advocating the use of a flotation device. The methods used in this beginner's course allow the pupil considerable freedom and comfort. It is highly desirable that he jump into the water, turn, roll over on his back and then on his stomach to rest, thrash about. All these actions help to familiarize him with the feel of water and with his personal reaction to it. That would be impossible without the aid of a flotation device, which eliminates his natural fear of not being able to stay afloat. The device offers enough buoyancy so that all the child's energies are available to propel him through the water, making advancement faster.

There are a number of good, inexpensive flotation devices available at most sporting goods stores. However, we have had great success with our "homemade" device. Our flotation device is made from a one-gallon can, unused, or one which formerly held varnish, olive oil, or gasoline. In order to secure a rope or tie to each end of the tin can, it is necessary to have another handle opposite the one already attached. This can be fashioned from a section of wire coat hanger. A piece six or seven inches long will suffice. It should be bent to resemble the handle at the top, then securely soldered to the bottom of the can. The rope is then looped through both handles.

The flotation device is placed on the youngster's back and

length away, your hands below the surface and extended toward the boy. Instructor and pupil are holding hands. In effect, the instructor's hands are like the handlebars of his boy's tricycle, which he can hold on to.

All these steps are necessary to maintain the boy's upright balance and build his confidence. The instructor must also keep reassuring him that he won't let go of his hands, and that absolutely nothing is going to happen—except some fun in the water. In time the boy himself will begin to release the pressure of his grip on the instructor's hands.

TRAINING TIPS FOR DAD

As your son starts to realize that he will not tip over or sink, his first normal fears will abate. Suggest to him that he can remain upright even when he is holding on with one hand. If he expresses doubts, *don't* rush him into the move! Sooner or later he will loosen his grip on one of your hands. That has happened in just about every case. And when he does let go, praise him. There—he can stay afloat one-handed!

Switch hands, letting him hold on to the one he had previously released, while grasping the other hand firmly. Eventually, the time will come when he dares experiment by releasing both hands. The youngster will have taken a large step forward in conquering his fears and will be on the road to swimming at last. Of course, he still has a long way to go, but confidence in his own ability is of paramount importance at this stage of learning.

Now that the young pupil has learned that he will not

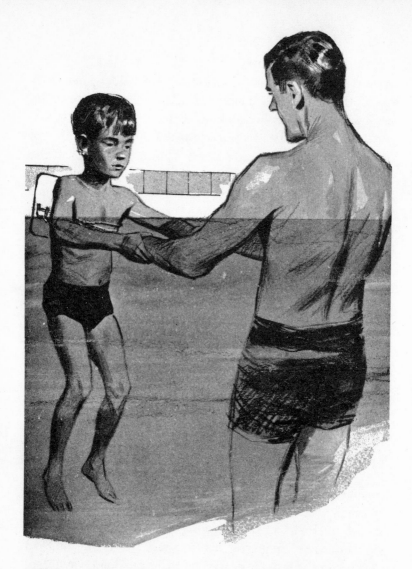

Building confidence in your son is a step-by-step process. Let him grip both your wrists at first. Later, as he becomes accustomed to the water, encourage him to let go with one hand. Notice that his back is only inches from the wall of the pool, insurance that he won't tip forward in the water.

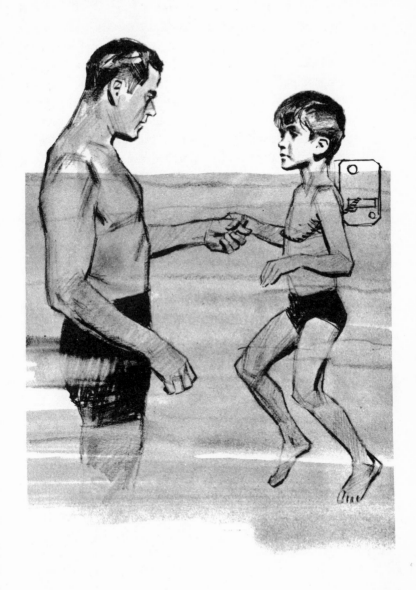

sink while the flotation device is on his back, Dad and son can switch places, with Dad's back against the side of the pool and the youngster facing him, his back to the deeper water. At this point the lad has sufficient room to begin moving his legs (had he begun the leg movement earlier, perhaps he might have kicked his feet against the side of the pool).

Dad should instruct him to move his legs as if he were walking or riding a tricycle; not with great effort, as running or pedaling fast, but firmly, easily, naturally, with a good, strong, steady gait. This will help to improve his already-improving balance.

Moving About in an Upright Position

To give the youngster the feel of moving through the water, the first step is simple enough: the instructor holds the pupil by the hands, and, walking backward slowly, pulls him along. The boy's legs continue the firm, steady bicycling motion to give him additional stability.

Next comes the youngster's first basic arm movement, which will lead to the dog-paddle stroke. Instruct the boy to reach his arms ahead slightly and "paw in the water," just as if he were a dog digging in the sand. He is, in effect, grabbing little cupped handfuls of water.

To permit him to accomplish this without obstruction, the instructor stands in front of the pupil, and, reaching out, holds the boy's chin in his hand. As the boy moves forward, the instructor steps backward. The boy should have plenty of room to reach ahead in his pawing movement.

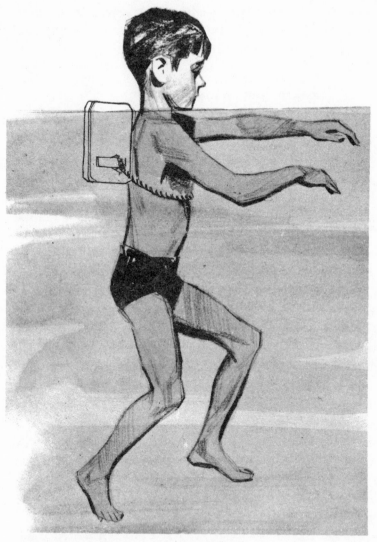

Well balanced in the water. The "bicycle" movement of the legs affords added stability, helping the boy stay erect with little effort.

What the lad will have accomplished is a first attempt at *connected arm-and-leg movement*. Of course, it isn't coordinated, and undoubtedly there will be some splashing, but that's to be expected.

TRAINING TIPS FOR DAD

Now you can show your son that the combination of the flotation device, leg action, and the digging movement of the hands can actually propel him through the water. By holding him under the chin and walking backward, you have proved that he is quite capable of moving forward. After practicing this a few times, you can slowly remove your hand, and the chin support should be dispensed with. In a short time he should be able to move in this *erect position* for any reasonable distance.

As confidence and capability grow, these exercises can be turned into a series of games. One such game is Chase-Me Tag. Use a "playing field" at the shallow end of the pool, leaving yourself some room to move around, and let the lad come "walking" after you. Another good game is Follow the Leader. Dad can walk a zigzag course in the shallow end of the pool, trying all sorts of antics, such as making waves and shaking his head from side to side. A third game is Shove the Kickboard. (More about the kickboard in a succeeding chapter.) Using the walking technique, your son pushes the kickboard ahead of him. He walks after it, then shoves it forward again. All these games are quite simple and natural, and Dad can invent a few more at any time. All games should be designed to give the boy added confidence, to let him splash around, to instill in him the idea that it's *fun* to be in a swimming pool.

Sooner or later, your boy may want to climb out of the pool, and then leap back into the water, while you stand there to see that nothing goes amiss. All youngsters are naturally adventurous. Once they see what they can do—performing feats that were once all but insurmountable in

Jumping from the side of the pool is fun and will help your son gain confidence.

their impressionable minds—they delight in repeating their new trick over and over again.

Dad must always laud the boy. Praise from father is, in many ways, almost as important as performance of the feat itself.

2

Dog Paddle

The basic stroke taught to a child by most swimming instructors is called the dog paddle, or human stroke. For many teachers, as well as for their pupils, it is the easiest form of swimming because it does not involve timing and coordination between the arm stroke and the leg kick.

The term "human stroke" is used because it is so basically natural. The position of the body and the movement of the arms and legs are, in many ways, similar to the ones used by the youngster early in life as he crawled across the floor. The arm actions and the position of the head are exactly the same. The alternating movement of each arm and leg is also similar; the leg motion is only slightly different, in that there is less hip flexion (bending) and the legs are extended out more. This form of swimming is extremely simple and can be learned by children in the lower age group.

Up to this point the child has *not* been swimming, regardless of the fact that he has succeeded in moving about in the water. In fact, he has not even been in *swimming position*, for he has been erect, his head out of the water, his legs hanging down vertically.

The first step, walking through water, was useful for two reasons: First, it helped build confidence in the beginner, for he found that he could remain afloat; he lost his fear of being in the water at a depth where his feet did not

Beginning to learn the dog paddle. The boy's body is tipped forward at a 45-degree angle. The bicycling motion of the legs and the pawing, digging motion of his slightly cupped hands continue.

touch bottom. Second, it introduced him to the idea of treading water, which is the "rest period" used by all swimmers when they feel tired. He learned how to move his hands and bicycle his legs to keep afloat.

The first step toward the dog paddle is begun from the erect position in the water. The child tips his body forward at an angle of approximately 45 degrees. As he does so, his legs will almost automatically rise commensurately. The arm-and-leg action continues as before. The hands reach out to grasp the little handfuls of water, the legs move as though walking or riding a bicycle. The only basic difference is the angle of the body in the water. Finally, the beginner assumes the crawling position so familiar to his childhood. The head is erect, he is on his stomach, the arm-and-leg action continues.

To all intents and purposes, the pupil is now *actually swimming*. He is using the dog-paddle stroke to propel himself around the pool. The entire first lesson in true swimming, from erect position to the dog-paddle stroke, is usually accomplished fairly quickly.

TRAINING TIPS FOR DAD

When your child first attempts the final dog-paddle position, he may be fearful that his face will drop below the surface. The exercise used previously—standing in front of him and cupping your fingers under his chin—can be used profitably again. In time he'll get the hang of it, in that astonishing, quick-learning way all boys and girls seem to have.

After your son has gained sufficient experience and confidence executing the dog paddle with the flotation device, encourage him to try it without the flotation on his back. By holding him under the chin, you will help to keep his face above the surface of the water, and also give him the security of knowing you are there to help if necessary. In time, he will ask you to let him try without your help.

The question that arises in the minds of many parents is, "When can I allow my son to do the dog paddle without the flotation device?" I have found that in nearly all cases, the child himself determines the proper time. When he has gained sufficient confidence in his ability to stay afloat, he will let you know. However, if he does not make that decision himself, you should encourage him to try it. You might let him remove the flotation; then ease him into the water, and, holding him under the chin, let him try the arm-and-leg actions of the dog paddle. In time he will ask you to let go, so that he can try moving under his own power.

One of the most important steps to instill confidence in the youngster is to have him jump into deep water from the side of the pool, or the diving board, with the device on. However, should he attempt that, make sure you are there, standing in the water or at the edge of the pool. Your presence will reassure him.

And it is a proud moment for father and son when that five-year-old navigates about in the dog paddle on his own. Heap on the praise! It is an accomplishment that can be shared, one that will remain in the memory of the child—and the adult—for many years to come.

3

Submerging the Head
and Floating

The dog paddle has taught the beginner to move about
through the water in rudimentary fashion. In his introduction to swimming, he has held his head above the surface
of the water. From this point, in order to progress to the
crawl stroke, it will be necessary for him to submerge his
face, so that he can learn *controlled breathing*, with his
mouth and nose under water. Controlled breathing simply
means that air is inhaled when the mouth and nose are out
of the water and exhaled when the mouth and nose are
under water.

Actually, most children learn to cope with water on the
face and head at an early age. They splash about in the bath-
tub, and out of curiosity often lower their faces near or to
the surface of the water. Later, when they are old enough
to take showers, a cascade of water surrounds the entire
head. Shampooing the hair has undoubtedly added to the
child's familiarity with water flowing around the head, nose,

Submerging the face and "blowing bubbles" is fun for youngsters. Remember, Dad, encourage him to keep his eyes open while his face is below the surface of the water.

mouth, and chin. He has discovered that there is nothing particularly frightening about water as such, especially after his first experience with the dog paddle. Nor is there anything mysterious about holding one's breath. No doubt the average child has experimented with breath control without realizing it, since he first puffed out his cheeks and held his breath. Therefore, the introduction to controlled breathing simply requires the child to put the two factors together: submerging the face while holding his breath.

The initial lesson can be practiced at home. A dishpan or washbasin filled about halfway with clear, cool water is needed. The pupil takes a deep breath, holds it, puts his face in the water, counts to three (or four or five, depending on his whim), and then removes his face from the dishpan.

Once the child has accomplished that first step and practiced it a few times, the next action is the release of the breath while the nose and mouth are under water. That too is quite simple. He merely blows out through his mouth. When all the air has been expelled, he comes up for another breath. Most children are fascinated by the way they are "blowing bubbles" under water.

Perhaps the one difficulty that may be encountered lies in prevailing upon the child to keep his eyes open while his face is submerged. There are two basic reasons why this is necessary: First, the swimmer should always know where he's going. Second is the psychological aspect, particularly for a beginner. When the youngster can see everything that is going on about him, fear of an unfamiliar element will vanish.

TRAINING TIPS FOR DAD

Concentrate on proper inhaling and exhaling first. The pupil should learn to breathe in and out almost exclusively through his mouth. Explain to him that this method of breathing helps to keep water out of the nasal passages.

After your son has experienced this breathing technique and can execute it while his face is submerged, try timing his breath control. Whereas he kept his face submerged for perhaps five seconds, increase the count to six, seven, eight, or more, until he has gained confidence in his ability to hold his face under water for as much as ten seconds without fear or discomfort.

Most children tend to wipe their eyes after removing the face from the water, to get rid of the droplets clinging to eyebrows and eyelashes. Instruct your boy to refrain from using his hands. Instead, have him squeeze his eyelids together tightly, then open his eyes quickly. He'll get used to this technique in a surprisingly short time.

Teaching the beginner to keep his eyes open under water is really simpler than might be imagined. I recommend an exercise that has proved quite successful: have your son jump into the water and then look for you. You can be submerged yourself, or you can move around to different parts of the pool while he is under water. The more he does this, the quicker he will get used to the idea.

I also recommend as a training tip that the boy cling to the side of the pool and then lower his head below the surface.

One of the most popular exercises, used by many instructors in teaching children to keep their eyes open, is the "penny-and-poker-chip" approach. This game can be practiced in the pool, or at home while using the basin of water. All it requires is a few coins of different denomination, buttons, and poker chips. While the boy closes his eyes (or turns his head) Dad slips something into the water. The boy ducks his face and sees what is lying on the bottom: penny, dime, button, chip, or quarter.

FLOATING

Webster's Dictionary offers the following definition of swimming: "To move through the water by moving arms, legs and fins; to move along smoothly; to float on or in a liquid. . . ." That is truly an accurate definition of what a swimmer does. He floats in water and moves smoothly along by the action of legs and arms. Of course, there is more to it than that. *Proper* swimming, especially when executing the crawl stroke, means *coordination* of floating, leg action and arm movement, and controlled breathing.

The Prone Float

Most human bodies are naturally buoyant and can float in a number of positions, including face-up and face-down. The one that is used in the crawl stroke is the face-down position, often referred to as the "prone float." The floater practices this phase of swimming while moving through the water, or while remaining relatively motionless.

Standing in shallow water, the boy takes a deep breath, holds it, and extends his arms forward so that his biceps are alongside his ears. Then he leans forward, pushing ahead with his toes from the bottom of the pool. His legs will float up, and he will be lying comfortably in the water, his body in a horizontal plane. To recover, he simply stands up by bending at the hips and dropping his feet to the bottom of the pool.

The floater will travel a greater distance if he can manage to push off from the side of the pool. By using that technique the power of the legs can be brought into play, and the floater will glide forward several body lengths. Standing in shallow water, the floater can begin by balancing momentarily on one foot and placing the sole of his other foot against the side of the pool. He proceeds as previously, taking a deep breath, bending forward to the water, then pushing ahead, using the foot that was braced against the side of the pool.

Later, as the boy practices, he will be able to reach a point of familiarity with floating whereby he can push off with both feet, increasing the length of his forward glide. These exercises will indicate to him how freely the body can move through the water when kept in a streamlined position.

TRAINING TIPS FOR DAD

You can assist in familiarizing your son with the feeling of a forward glide. Have him take a deep breath and then bend forward. Grasp his outstretched hands, and, as he lies down in the water, you walk backward, pulling him along. When his breath is spent and he lifts his head, help him stand up. Later, he can stand up by himself, bending at the waist and dropping his feet to the bottom of the pool.

Once he has learned the technique of shoving off from the side of the pool, challenge him to "float over to you." Extend the distance foot by foot, until he can glide forward a considerable (for him) distance. These exercises will not only increase his confidence but also, to some extent, build up his breath capacity.

4

The Crawl Stroke

The crawl stroke, which is taught to the youngster as he progresses to an advanced form of swimming, is in every way the same style used by our champions. When a child shows that he is ready to advance (which is after he can execute the prone float) there is no reason to teach any other method.

The manner of kicking the legs and the movement of the arms, as well as the proper breathing, must be taught with the same attention to detail which would be used in coaching someone who is able to swim to a championship degree. Any early mistakes developed in a youngster's stroke might continue throughout his swimming career and retard his chances for excellence.

THE LEG KICK

The movement of the legs in the crawl stroke accomplishes two basic purposes: it helps to propel the swimmer through the water, and it gives balance to the whole body while the arm action is in progress.

Inexperienced swimmers, or those who have not been taught properly, misunderstand what the kicking motion really does. They think that as long as the legs are moving, thrashing about and kicking hard, then they are accomplishing their purpose. Nothing could be further from the truth! There is a correct way and an incorrect way to execute the leg kick. Using an incorrect kick, the swimmer will splash in the water, tire himself out, and make little forward progress. Using a proper kicking action, the swimmer will move farther, faster, and with less effort.

The Leg Action

Basically, the legs are applying pressure against the water in order to achieve forward propulsion. When the leg is moving downward, water is being forced *down and backward* by the front of the leg, the knee and the instep of the foot. When the leg is moving upward, water is being forced *upward and backward* by the back of the leg and the sole of the foot.

In executing the crawl kick, the movement of the leg originates in the hip joint, in an up-and-down fashion. The knees bend slightly. The ankles are loose, with the toes pointed slightly in, almost as if the swimmer were pigeon-toed.

Beginners often make the error of bending the knees too much during the kick. That causes the legs to lose their "grip" on the water.

The Leg Position

During the crawl kick motion, one leg is moving up as the other is moving down. It is vital that both legs be close together. The knees should almost brush against each other as they pass; barely an inch should separate them.

Depth of the Kick

The kicker's foot should not lift above the surface of the water on the upkick. If any part of the foot does break the surface, it should be very slightly.

The length of the downward kick depends on such factors as the length of the swimmer's legs and the most comfortable extension of the leg. As a rule, a kick should be roughly twelve inches from toe to heel. A longer kick is not necessary, for it wastes power and might destroy timing. A short kick, which does nothing more than produce vibration, may not provide sufficient power for good forward propulsion and might also upset the timing.

Rhythm of the Kick

Most coaches and swimming instructors agree that the six-beat kick rhythm is the most nearly correct and should be taught if at all possible.

It is a relatively simple thing, as the legs move up and down alternately, to say silently: "LEFT (one-two-three),

RIGHT (one-two-three)" in a steady, even count. Practicing this "balanced" kicking will be helpful for later synchronization with arm action and controlled breathing.

TRAINING TIPS FOR DAD

Even before your son attempts to execute the proper leg action in the water, a dry-land drill is helpful.

Have your son lie across his bed, face down, so that his body, from the hips down dangles off the bed. In this manner you can observe his leg movements closely. The drill is designed to establish leg control and teach correct leg action.

See to it that the movement originates from the hips, that there is only a small amount of knee bend, that the ankles are relaxed and turned in somewhat, so that the feet are slightly pigeon-toed. Check on the leg position during the kick: the knees should be passing each other about an inch apart. If your son shows a tendency to begin separating his legs, instruct him to think in terms of his toes. The big toes of both feet should almost graze each other as the legs move alternately up and down.

The following method can be used to control the depth of your son's kick: place your right arm over his legs and your left arm under his legs, with both your arms about twelve to fourteen inches apart. Your arms thus prevent him from kicking any higher or lower than necessary.

Once you are satisfied that the boy has learned the technique of the kick on dry land, he can practice in the pool. Have the boy hang on to the side of the pool and extend his body out into the water. He can practice balanced kicking in this position as you stand to one side, close to his legs, observing the leg action. Any errors, such as rigid action of the ankles, bending the knees too much, inadvertently spreading the legs apart, or a kick with too much depth, can be corrected.

When you are satisfied that your son has made sufficient progress in his poolside kicking drills, he can be allowed to use his leg action to propel himself through the water. This is accomplished through the use of a kickboard, which is simply a piece of buoyant plastic foam, about fourteen to sixteen inches wide and twenty-four inches long, that will keep your son afloat in a swimming position for the kicking drill. It is very inexpensive, not easily damaged, and can be purchased at virtually any department, toy, or sporting goods store.

Moving through the water with the aid of a kickboard is a useful drill at all stages of the swimmer's development. Notice that the knees bend only slightly. On the upkick, the heel barely breaks the surface of the water. Toes are pointed in somewhat. Feet are not more than twelve to fourteen inches apart, knees close together.

Holding on to the kickboard, your son simply lies comfortably in the water, then uses the leg action to move about. He can easily steer it—youngsters learn how to do that by themselves very quickly. With the aid of the kickboard the lad should be able to propel himself ahead with surprising speed if the leg action is correct.

The kickboard is *never* dispensed with. It is used not only as a method of training, but it is also invaluable for the daily practice so necessary in the development of leg strength.

ARM MOVEMENTS

Although the leg kick plays an important role in moving the swimmer through the water, it is the arm movement that supplies most of the propulsion. Proper arm movement is extremely important, and requires a great deal of practice, in both the dry-land and water drills.

As has been pointed out, the leg kick helps provide propulsion by exerting pressure against the water. The same thing is true of the arm action. In a manner of speaking, the palm of the hand and the inside part of the arm are "pushing backward" on the water.

The arm action in the crawl stroke can be divided into four parts: First is the *entry*, which is the way the hand and arm enter the water. Next is the *power thrust*, and this can be divided into two parts: the *pull* of the arm, from the point of entry into the water and as it moves under the body, and the *push* of the arm, from the stomach area on backward, as it pushes the water backward. Finally, the fourth part of the arm action is the *recovery*, which means taking the arm out of the water in order to begin another stroke with the arm.

Entry

To begin the stroke, the arm is extended forward, straight ahead, directly in line with the shoulder. The fingers should be close together and relaxed, but *not limp*. The palm should be slightly cupped.

The fingertips dip into the water. When the hand is below the surface, the swimmer should feel the pressure of the water against his slightly cupped hand. Just as a paddle puts pressure against the water, shoving it backward so that the boat can go forward, the cupped hand and inside of the arm push the water backward so the swimmer can go forward. If the paddle "slips" so that its broad side is not pushing the water back, there will be less propulsion. The same thing will happen if the arm action slips.

The Power Stroke

Once the entry has been accomplished, the hand and arm begin to exert pressure on the water, pushing it backward.

In the initial stage of the power stroke, the hand, wrist, and arm should be in a line. The wrist should be firm but not rigid, for if the wrist were relaxed it would tend to bend backward during the stroke, with resulting loss of power.

As the arm moves in its downward course, it begins to bend slightly, so that it will pass under the swimmer's stomach.

Many swimmers—even those who have achieved some small degree of proficiency—think that the arm, wrist, and hand should always be in a line, that the sweep of the arm should always be alongside the body. That is not quite accurate.

The swimmer is trying to push the water back *from under his body*. In order to do that, the *arm itself* must be somewhat under the center of the body. This technique adds greatly to the power and forward propulsion of the swimmer.

As the arm passes under the stomach, it begins to move outward again, still continuing to exert pressure against the water. At the conclusion of the stroke, the hand should be alongside the body, with the thumb almost brushing against the swimmer's thigh.

The arm stroke, during its power thrust, has been described in detail, from the in-a-line entry to the slight bend of the elbow as the arm comes under the stomach and through the straightening of the elbow as the hand almost touches the swimmer's thigh. But there must be no "hitch," no hesitation in the over-all movement. The entire stroke must be accomplished in one smooth operation.

Recovery

Lifting the arm out of the water should be done effortlessly. As the power stroke is completed, the elbow begins to bend. The arm is lifted out of the water quickly and smoothly, with the elbow bent, the forearm and upper arm almost at right angles to each other. Then the swimmer reaches his arm forward, wrist and arm in a line, for the next arm stroke.

TRAINING TIPS FOR DAD

Just as the leg action was first practiced with a dry-land drill, so can the arm movement. It will be very helpful if your son can practice in front of a full-length mirror, so that he, as well as you, can observe his actions.

Standing in front of the mirror, his upper body bent over, the boy can begin his step-by-step practice. The entry is first, the arm, wrist, and hand in a line. To impress upon him the exact action, have him exaggerate the movement a bit by causing him to rub the inside of his upper arm against his ear as he begins the stroke. Naturally, he won't necessarily be brushing his arm against his ear while actually swimming, but this drill is intended to give him the general idea of the arm position. He will adjust it when he is in the water.

Check on the arm action during the power thrust: the slight bend of the elbow to allow his arm to pass under his stomach, the straightening of the arm as it moves toward the back of the body, the brushing of the thumb against the outside of the thigh as the stroke is completed.

Perhaps your son might have a tendency to lift his arm higher than necessary for the recovery. Explain that he is simply lifting the hand and arm clear of the water to begin another entry. Shoulder and upper arm should be more or less in a line, with the forearm at right angles to the upper arm. This will allow for plenty of room to start the stroke without wasting power or energy in beginning the new stroke.

The first practice in the water can be executed in the

D

Two good dry-land drills. Standing in front of a mirror, your son (and Dad) can check the proper arm movements. By exaggerating the arm movement and having the boy rub his upper arm against his ear at the beginning of the stroke, he will get the general idea of the arm action. (See also opposite page.)

face-down, or prone, float position. Taking his deep breath and holding it, your son begins to move through the water, using the previously practiced leg kick and the arm action to propel himself forward. There need be no attempt at coordination of arms and legs, nor should controlled breathing be introduced at this point. The technique of the kick and the arm action should be practiced. Coordination can come later.

Practicing while lying prone on a small table or ironing board allows your son to get the feel of the stroke while in the prone position.

BREATH CONTROL

Fitting controlled breathing into the crawl stroke requires that the swimmer learn to execute *rhythmically*. This means he will be doing it "by the numbers."

The pupil begins by taking a breath and plunging his face into the water, and, as he does so, he begins to exhale. When his breath is completely expelled, he does *not* raise his head to remove it from the water; instead, he *rotates*

Proper breath control, coordinated with arm and leg action, takes plenty of practice. Note that the boy's eyes are open. Air is taken in through the open mouth as the head rotates in the water.

his head (left or right, whichever position is most comfortable for him) so that one ear and the side of his face remain in the water, but his nose and mouth are above the surface. Another breath is taken in, and the face is rotated back so that nose and mouth are submerged again. The procedure is repeated.

At this point it should be quite clear why it was so important that the hands be kept away from the face when it came out of the water. While swimming, the youngster would have no opportunity to brush the water droplets from his eyes. The quick, hard squint will do the job just as well and leave his hands free to do the job of stroking.

TRAINING TIPS FOR DAD

This phase of breath control can be practiced at home with the basin of water. Of course, it can also be practiced at the pool. Have your son hold on to the side of the pool, extending his body outward. He can practice the rotation of the head by moving his face from the surface to its underwater position and back to the surface.

COORDINATING ARMS, LEGS AND BREATH CONTROL

The crawl stroke is a combination of leg kick, arm movement, and breath control. Putting these components together is not as difficult as one would think. For the most part it is a matter of practice.

Before delving deeper into the proper technique of co-ordination, let me point out that I advocate the *four-stroke cycle* between breaths. In the early stages of learning, a mistake made by breathing after every two strokes may become hard to break. And I have made it a rule never to practice mistakes. Breathing every four strokes allows the child to think about his next move.

Now, let us first assume that the pupil feels more natural when he breathes with the left side of his face out of the water. In that case he should set up his rhythm by starting to stroke first with his left arm. The face is submerged. With a steady movement he begins: "Left stroke, right stroke, left stroke, right stroke . . ." On that fourth stroke, taken with the right arm, the head rotates so that a breath can be taken.

The pupil will notice that as he turns for a breath, the body rolls slightly on its long axis. In other words, it is rolling a bit to the right, with the right shoulder and the right side of the body a little deeper in the water.

Just before the left side of the face emerges from the water, air should be forced *out* through the mouth. Then, as the left side of the face emerges, air should be drawn *in*. The body rolls back again to its level line as the next stroke, with the left arm, is taken.

During the movement with the arms and head, the legs should be kicking up and down rhythmically, smoothly. It is possible that some naturally rhythmic youngsters might fall into the six-beat kick almost immediately, but with most pupils that won't happen right away. However, this should cause no concern. As long as the kicking continues approximately in that rhythm, with a steady action, the correct rhythm will eventually fall into place.

During the initial phase of instruction, Dad must be right there, ready to spot any mistakes and correct them as soon as possible.

TRAINING TIPS FOR DAD

During the four-stroke cycle, while your son is moving ahead with his face submerged, the water should be about on a level with his hairline. Check on that by standing in front of him as he swims toward you.

When he rotates his head to take a breath, the boy might raise his head too much or roll too far. Instruct him to rotate his head just enough so that the nose and mouth are out of the water.

Remember, Dad, this is the time to spot and correct any errors. Don't let your son practice his mistakes!

During these training sessions, while correcting your son's technique, he may feel tired or irritated with continued practice and instruction. Don't press the boy! If he's tired, let him rest. If he says he's had enough for one day, so be it. After all, swimming is fun, not a chore. Some youngsters get the hang of it sooner than others. Over the long haul, your son will learn to swim just as well as any other boy who is given similar instruction. It is as important for the instructor to show patience and understanding as it is for the pupil to learn.

5

The Backstroke

The backstroke should be the next swimming challenge for your son. There are a number of similarities between the backstroke and the crawl stroke. In fact, some coaches call it an "upside-down crawl," or "a crawl stroke executed on one's back." The leg kick resembles the crawl kick in some respects, and there is an alternating arm action. The six-beat rhythm is also the same.

In one way, the backstroke is easier to execute than the crawl, because the swimmer's face is always above the surface, and therefore there is no problem with breath control. But in another aspect it is more difficult, since it is harder to achieve good body position in the water. Nevertheless, anyone who can learn the crawl should encounter little difficulty in progressing satisfactorily with the backstroke.

Floating

Obviously, the beginner should learn to float properly on his back before attempting to propel himself backward through the water. For the first few lessons, the flotation device will prove useful. It should be worn so that the can sits comfortably on the swimmer's chest and upper stomach. Normally, it is quite difficult to float motionless on one's back, for the legs and upper thighs have a tendency to drop, thus pulling the floater down into the water. With a flotation device the pupil need not worry about that.

In proper position, the floater's back should be slightly arched, his legs straight, and his ears covered by the water.

It should also be remembered that floating is made easier when there is air in the lungs, which means that exhaling should be done rapidly and another breath taken immediately.

Leg Action

First, it would be wise to examine the points of similarity between the leg actions of the crawl and backstroke.

In both, the kick is initiated primarily by a hip action. In both, pressure is exerted against the water by parts of the feet and legs, except that the backstroke action is the reverse of the crawl. In the backstroke kick, on the downward motion of the leg, pressure is exerted against the water by the sole of the foot and the back of the leg. This forces the water down and backward. On the upkick, the instep and shin force the water upward and backward. The action is primarily under the surface of the water, with the toes barely coming to the surface.

The difference between the two kicks is in the knee bend. There is more flexion of the knee on the downward kick in the backstroke. The knee is straightened for the upward kick.

Arm Movement

Like the crawl stroke, the backstroke uses an alternating arm action. How far back should the arm reach? That is difficult to judge exactly, for it depends to a great extent on how far back the youngster can reach. Ideally, the arm should enter the water when it is straight, just a little bit *after* it passes a straight-out extension from the shoulder, moving toward the head.

The power thrust in the backstroke is different from that in the crawl. Now the arm acts as the oar of a rowboat, dipping into the water to a depth of eight or nine inches. Then the palm of the hand and the inside of the arm push the water backward, toward the feet. The arm moves nearly parallel to the surface of the water.

When the hand reaches a point where it is alongside the thigh, it is removed from the water, then moved in a shallow arc toward the point of entry.

As with the crawl stroke, the body will roll slightly downward as the arm enters the water. As the left arm enters, the body will roll a bit downward on the left side; the same action takes place when the right arm enters the water.

TRAINING TIPS FOR DAD

Start your son on his backstroke training program with a dry-land drill. You can use a narrow table or cot, or an ironing board is a good substitute.

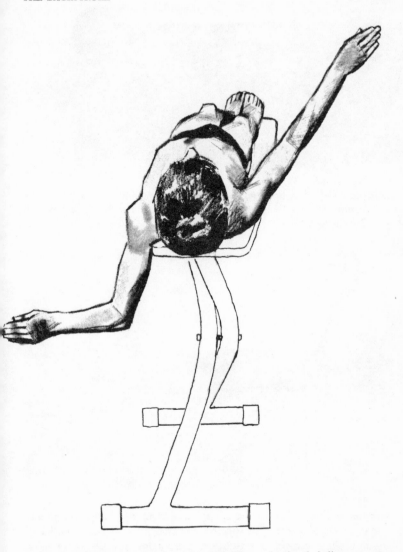

A narrow table or ironing board is ideal for a dry-land drill to practice the backstroke arm action. Using this method, your son can spot-check his own arm movements.

Dad can help the boy get accustomed to moving backward in the water through the hand-under-neck technique. He moves backward, pulling the boy.

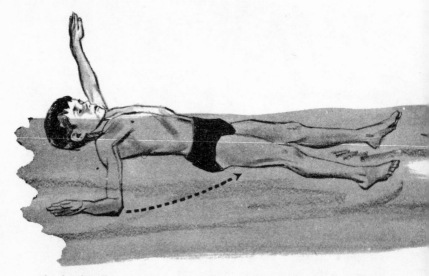

The backstroke in action. Note the position of the body, lying comfortably in the water. The stroking arm moves in a line parallel to the body; the recovering arm moves in a shallow arc toward re-entry. The leg action is somewhat similar to the crawl kick, but with a bit more knee bend.

Have your son lie down on the table or cot so that his legs dangle off the edge. He should be supported only to the bottom of his buttocks, to allow for free kicking action. It might be helpful if a book is inserted between the table and the small of his back, in order to indicate to him that his back should be slightly arched. In this position he can begin to practice the arm and leg movements.

To coach him in the proper leg kick, grasp his ankles and guide his legs through the correct motions: feet slightly turned in, with a strong hip action.

Use the same technique for the arm movement. During the dry-land drill, your son can observe for himself what he might not be able to see or feel while he is in the water: that the arm moves outward in a rather shallow position and that the arm is straight until it passes just past the shoulder, when the elbow bends slightly and the arm continues on toward the leg. There should be a definite *pushing away* of the water with the palm of the hand. The hand acts as if it were the blade of an oar.

When moving your son on his back for the first time, it is important that you help him feel comfortable in the water. Even with the flotation device resting reassuringly on his stomach, the boy may need some additional assistance, if for no other reason than to keep his confidence.

Stand behind him with your hand placed under the nape of his neck. As you move backward, pull him along. Instruct him to move his arms and flutter his legs. When the flotation is removed and the boy tries it alone, it would still be a good idea to use the hand-under-neck aid.

Later, when your son tries to "solo," you might notice that

he is moving his arms too rapidly. This is normal and is due to a fear of sinking, but with experience the rapidity will diminish into a normal stroke.

If the boy has made satisfactory progress in the crawl stroke, coordinating the six-beat backstroke rhythm should present no problem. All it takes is confidence and practice.

As was mentioned previously, breathing is not much of a problem in the backstroke. Air is taken in as needed. However, as has been cited several times in this book, the body is naturally more buoyant when there is air in the lungs, so that exhaling and inhaling should be performed quickly.

6

The Breast Stroke

The breast stroke is one of the oldest methods of swimming known to man. In some sections of the world it is considered the beginner's stroke. It is quite likely that humans learned to execute this stroke by watching frogs navigate through the water, for the movements of the arms and legs in this stroke do bear a vague resemblance to the movements of a frog, and for that reason the leg action is usually described as a "frog kick."

In general, the *recreational* breast stroke requires less effort and energy by the swimmer, but in competition, the energy requirements are the same as for the other strokes. However, regardless of which type of swimming is attempted (recreational or competition), the breast stroke is more easily perfected than learned. A youngster with a natural frog kick will get the hang of it quickly, while a child who does not have that same natural kick will be much slower to learn.

The movement of the legs in the breast-stroke kick is so

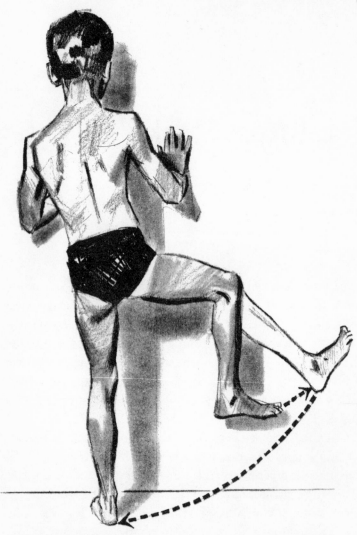

A good basic method to learn the fundamentals of the frog kick. The inside of the knee and ankle touch the wall, with the knee bent so that the thigh and lower leg form a 90-degree angle. Then, with the leg raised slightly, the foot kicks back to position alongside the other foot.

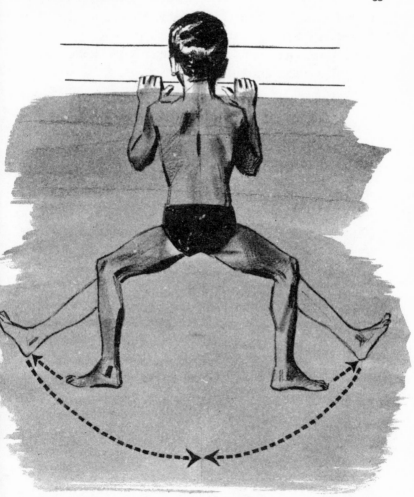

The frog kick as practiced in the pool. Holding on to the side of the pool, in a vertical position, with his body along the wall, the boy executes the kick as in the dry-land drill, this time with both legs simultaneously. He should feel the water pressure against the inside of the foot, leg, and thigh.

E

different from all other leg kicks that it is best to use a method that breaks down the action to its simplest form. Try this introduction, which will be given under the heading "Training Tips" as a dry-land drill.

The Breast-Stroke Kick (Frog Kick)

Have your son stand facing a wall about two or three inches from it. Instruct him to raise his right leg, bending it at the knee, so that the shin and thigh form a right angle. Then have him move his bent leg so that the *inside part* of the knee, leg, and ankle are touching the wall. That is a close

After sufficient practice, he can extend his body horizontally in the water, holding on to the side of the pool, continuing the exercise.

approximation of the position of the legs at the beginning of the frog kick.

Now have your son move his leg outward, until it is almost straight, and then have him bring it downward and parallel to the other.

After several attempts with one leg, let him try the other one. This simple at-home drill will surely show him that there is a difficult hip rotation as well as the need for the feet to turn outward and for a snap closing of the legs as they come together after every thrust.

The next step is practice in the water—not swimming, but a poolside exercise.

First, the pupil, while hanging on to the side of the pool, should practice assuming the same leg position, using the wall of the pool as he did the wall of his room at home. Once he has the positioning firmly fixed in his mind, he can extend his body out into the water, still holding onto the side of the pool for support.

When executing the kick correctly, the boy will feel the pressure of the water against the inside of the foot, leg, and thigh. He will also find that this correct kick will tend to force his body slightly upward.

One of the basic errors made by most beginners is the execution of a kick which is not symmetrical, with one leg making a move that allows the knee to drop and the foot to turn inward rather than outward. The principles governing this form of swimming make it clear that the kick must have an outward, rounding movement, with both legs moving simultaneously and symmetrically, so one must avoid the drop of the knee. This would completely defeat the basic fundamentals of the breast-stroke kick.

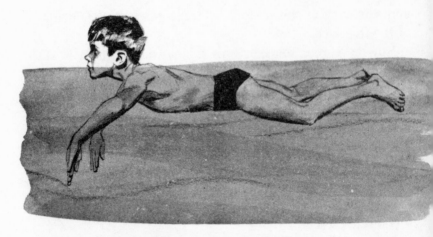

The arm action in the breast stroke. The arms are pulling out to execute a short stroke. Legs will then be drawn up. The swimmer takes a breath at this point.

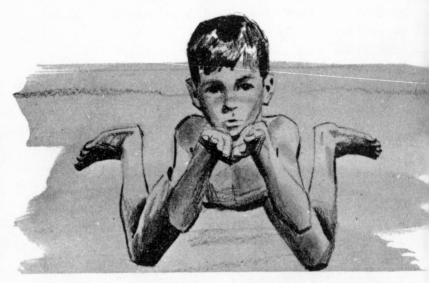

The breast stroke continues. Note that the arms have circled and the hands are under the chin, ready for forward thrust as the legs kick.

The Arm Action

The movement of the arms in the breast stroke can best be learned while the pupil is in the prone float position. The exercise begins with the swimmer lying comfortably in the water, arms extended forward, wrists turned inward. The index fingers of both hands are touching, the backs of the hands form an approximate 90-degree angle.

Now the arms execute a short, hard, outward pull. The key word here is *short*. Just before the arms reach a point where they are in line with the shoulders, the elbows bend and the hands come around under the chin and then move forward again, until the hands are extended forward in their original position.

As the arms move in the power stroke, the legs are drawn up slowly and smoothly to their "frog" position.

TRAINING TIPS FOR DAD

You can begin to coordinate the arm and leg movements of the breast stroke at this point, without worrying too much about breath control. That can come later.

Your son might better understand the basic actions of this stroke if you divide it into three parts:

1. As the arms pull out to execute the stroke, the legs are drawn up.
2. As the arms move around and forward again, the frog kick is executed.
3. There is a short glide.

Breath Control

The breath is taken in as the arms separate and move through the power stroke. The swimmer simply lifts his head until his mouth is clear of the water. He takes in air and then drops his head down into the water again as the frog kick is executed.

TRAINING TIPS FOR DAD

Proper coordination of arms, legs, and breathing is not as simple as it sounds. It requires a great deal of practice. It may be to your son's advantage that he do three series of arm-and-leg strokes before taking a breath. This method will allow him to concentrate on coordinating arm and leg movements, and since he will only be holding his breath for some ten or fifteen seconds, he should experience no discomfort.

All the above movements can be made even simpler if your boy makes his initial efforts while wearing the flotation device.

COMPETITION BREAST STROKE

Once the swimmer has become fairly proficient in the recreational breast stroke, he can begin to learn the technique used in competition. Over the years there have been some refinements in the breast stroke, which will help the swimmer move through the water faster. Basically, the alteration is in the leg kick.

The wide spread of the knees is eliminated. In order to narrow the movement and make for a more powerful kick, it is necessary to use a dry-land drill. As before, it can best be explained via training tips.

In the competition breast stroke, leg action in the frog kick is somewhat altered. Knees are not spread wide apart, the heels are near the buttocks. A good dry-land drill has the boy pushing his feet against Dad's hands.

TRAINING TIPS FOR DAD

Have your boy lie on the deck of the pool, arms outstretched over his head, legs about three inches apart, toes pointed outward. Instruct the boy to bend his knees so that his heels are near his buttocks. The knees should be rather together, not wide apart. Place your hands on the soles of his feet, the palms of your hands alongside his big toes. Now have him push out against your resisting hands.

This must be done over and over, until your son feels that his knees are being restricted from the wide, out-and-around thrust of the legs. The inside of the foot and the lower legs are the propellers. Probably the beginner's initial feeling will be that the new kick is less forceful than the recreational frog kick. But plenty of practice will prove its worth.

The arm action in the competition breast stroke is shortened and quickened. The long glide is eliminated. Breath is taken in at the beginning of the arm pull. If desired, the breath may be taken at every other stroke.

7

The Butterfly

In order to grasp the basic fundamentals of the butterfly, it is helpful to think of a dolphin. Anyone who has noted the way a dolphin's body undulates in a wavelike motion can readily understand what is required of a swimmer's body in the butterfly stroke. Of course, the swimmer has arms and the dolphin does not, but the arm action in this particular stroke is not difficult to learn.

It would be advantageous for both Dad and his son to witness the stroke being performed by someone who is accomplished in this form of swimming. A brief discussion, breaking down the movements in simple terms, will help to shorten the time it takes to grasp the body and arm movements. They will note that in the butterfly stroke the swimmer's body moves like a wave and that the arms recover simultaneously *over* the water, and are placed on the surface of the water about a shoulders' width apart.

The Body Action

To begin the instruction in proper body action, the swimmer should lie down in the prone float position, placing his arms at his sides. Taking a deep breath, he drops his head down into the water, making sure that his shoulders drop too. This movement automatically forces the hips to move upward.

As the hips come up toward the surface, the head is

Sequence showing how the undulating movement of the body is executed in the butterfly. After taking in air, the swimmer drops his head and shoulders, which brings the hips to the surface. Then (below) the head is lifted, and the lower legs and feet strike downward and backward against the water.

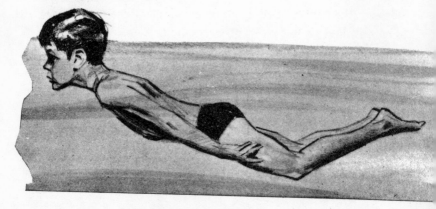

lifted. This series of movements produces the desired undulating effect and propels the body forward, for the lower legs and feet will also move, striking downward and backward against the water.

By practicing the body movement only, without bringing the arms into play, the swimmer will find himself moving across the pool with fairly good speed.

The Arm Movement

The swimmer starts in the prone float position, with his arms extended forward about a shoulders' width apart. Hands and arms then press strongly down and back, pushing the water backward under the body. The stroke is finished as the hands slide by the middle of the thighs. The recovery is made above the surface of the water. The arms reach forward again and return to their original position, extended forward about a shoulders' width apart.

Breath Control

As the arms begin their pull in the power stroke, the head is lifted so that the mouth may be open above the surface of the water. Air is taken in; then the head is dropped down into the water again as the arms finish their recovery.

TRAINING TIPS FOR DAD

Most of the practice should be in the body action, to attain the needed wavelike undulation. Remember, it starts at the head, radiates down through the body and hips, and ends with a good downward whip of the feet.

Instruct your son that when recovering, he must keep his

The finish of the butterfly stroke. The swimmer's arms have swept down and back, pushing the water backward under the body. Hands slide by the middle of the thighs; then the recovery stroke is made, with arms reaching forward for the next stroke. Note that the recovery is made with arms above the water.

palms down. When the hands are held in this position, there is less tension on the muscles of the upper arm.

Air can be taken in with every stroke, or every two strokes if desired.

It is also important to set up a good rhythm for the butterfly. Remember, as the arms reach forward and strike the water, the head is lowered. The head is lifted as the arms pull. This movement helps to continue the undulation and sets up the rhythm of the stroke.

8

The Side Stroke

The side stroke, although not a competition stroke, is still a useful method of swimming. Although it does not move the swimmer very rapidly through the water, it has a number of advantages.

First, because less physical energy is required, the side stroke helps the swimmer to rest, to take it easier, while still achieving some forward propulsion. Second, because the head is not submerged, there is no breath-control problem. And third, the side stroke is used to good advantage in lifesaving.

The side stroke should be learned after the pupil has become proficient in the competition strokes. By that time he will have a better understanding of proper balance in the water.

To begin the instruction, the swimmer should be lying comfortably in the water on his side and gliding through the water. (It does not matter which side; the most comfortable one for the swimmer is the best one.) The body is fully extended. The bottom arm is extended forward, and the top arm rests alongside the body.

The arm and leg movements must be made *simultaneously*. After a complete cycle of arm-and-leg movements, the body is back in the extended position.

The Leg Action

The legs work like a pair of scissors, opening and closing. To begin, the swimmer lies on the deck of the pool, on his side, body extended, with the bottom arm forward, top arm alongside the body.

Then the legs are flexed at the hip and extended backward. One leg (it can be top or bottom leg) is bent at the knee and extended forward. From this position the legs are whipped together, so that they are returned to a straight line, extended, with feet together.

The swimmer will feel the pressure of the water against the side and back of the bent leg as it kicks backward to its original extended position. Pressure will be felt on the top of the leg and the instep of the other leg as both legs scissor back to the extended position.

The Arm Action

The arm movement begins as the swimmer lies in the water on his side with his bottom arm extended and his top arm alongside the body. The two arms are brought together so that the fingertips meet at a point near the swimmer's chest. Then the top arm takes over the propulsion thrust, by moving back hard to full extension alongside the body. The bottom arm merely moves back, recovering, to full extended position ahead of the body.

The entire arm action should take place *below* the surface of the water.

TRAINING TIPS FOR DAD

Individually, the arm and leg actions are comparatively easy to learn. The only difficulty your son might encounter—and it is quickly overcome—is in the coordination of the arm and leg movements.

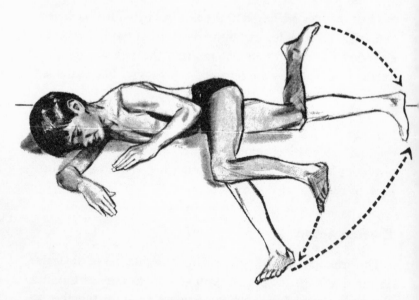

When the swimmer is executing the side-stroke kick, the legs open and close like a scissors. The top leg moves forward, the bottom leg is bent at the knee. Both legs kick together, then resume their original position for another leg kick.

The leg kick is executed while the top arm is thrusting back. In other words, as the hands begin to separate (after their fingertip meeting near the chest), with the lower arm extending forward and the top arm pushing the water back, the legs assist in the forward propulsion by executing the kick. This is a simple matter of timing and is not difficult to learn.

A dry-land drill will prove useful in practicing the synchronization of arms and legs. Instruct your son to lie on his side on the pool deck, his head resting on his extended lower arm, the top arm alongside his body. One leg should be bent and extended forward, the other leg also bent and extended to the rear. At the command "GO!" the arms should be moved, so that the fingertips meet parallel to, and not far from, his chest.

Now check to see the correctness of his arm-and-leg coordination. As the upper arm thrust is executed, so is the kick. As the arms draw together again for their fingertip meeting, the legs are flexed and moved into position for another kick.

Following the kick-and-thrust, there is a short glide forward before the arms and legs move into position to prepare for another kick-and-thrust.

F

9

Water Safety

It is hoped that by applying the methods described in this book, you and your children can enjoy a close relationship and participate safely in one of the finest of all sports, swimming. Although it is not the intention here to make *any* youngster competent in *all* water activities, since we are dealing with young people, and since it is possible that they may witness or become part of a water accident, it might be helpful to add a final chapter on a subject of paramount importance—water safety.

Many of the water accidents that take place at public beaches and pools are preventable, if only a few common-sense measures are applied. Some accidents are unavoidable, but an alert youngster who keeps his head can often assist in making a simple rescue.

The American Red Cross lists the three most frequent causes of accidental drowning as follows:

1. Failure to recognize and understand dangerous water conditions.

2. Lack of ability and/or training on the part of the swimmer, so that he is unable to escape a dangerous predicament once he finds himself in such a situation.

3. Unfamiliarity with useful methods and techniques when trying to come to the aid of swimmers in distress.

In order to cover the rules of water safety in a step-by-step manner, this chapter will be divided into three parts: (1) prevention of accidents in swimming and other sports; (2) useful measures when the swimmer is in a potentially dangerous situation; (3) artificial respiration.

PREVENTIVE MEASURES — SWIMMING

There are ten rules—a basic Ten Commandments, so to speak—which form the basis of practical water safety for swimmers:

1. Find out about water conditions before swimming in an area for the first time.

2. Don't race into the water the moment you arrive at the beach.

3. Don't swim in water that feels too cold.

4. When you begin to feel tired, get out of the water as soon as possible.

5. Avoid swimming in unfamiliar waters, especially when no lifeguard is on duty.

6. Never venture too far from shore, particularly at night, even if you are a good swimmer.

7. Use the buddy system. Try to have a friend (or Dad) with you whenever possible.

8. Avoid overeating before swimming.

9. Don't play rough in the water. Never duck anyone unexpectedly or hold someone's head under the surface.

10. Beginners should not venture far from shallow water.

Whenever possible, use the buddy system. If one swimmer encounters sudden, unexpected difficulty, the other is right there to help him.

There are good reasons for each rule. For example, water that is too cold may bring on muscle cramps. Tired muscles may also cramp or "knot up." A swimmer wading out into unfamiliar waters may not know about sudden drop-offs; there may be strong undercurrents at oceanside beaches that can pull a swimmer far from safety, and without a buddy nearby to lend a hand, the swimmer might be in serious difficulty. Ducking a person playfully and unexpectedly may cause him to swallow water and become ill.

Swimming is great fun. Preventive water safety can keep it enjoyable.

PREVENTIVE MEASURES — OTHER SPORTS

Boating

First, check the boat (or canoe) and its equipment. Does the craft leak? How many passengers can it safely hold? Is there a buoyant boat cushion or life jacket for each person aboard? If the boat has an outboard motor, are all connections tight? How much fuel is in the tank? Are there paddles ready for use in case the motor conks out? Is there a first-aid kit handy?

Boarding a small boat correctly is important. The best way is to step into it as close to the center as possible. Then, holding the sides, lower the body easily and sit down.

When the boat is moving, passengers should avoid changing positions unless absolutely necessary. If you must change your position, try to stay in the center of the boat, over its keel.

Canadian canoes should be paddled from a kneeling position for maximum safety.

In spite of all these precautions, it is possible that a boat or canoe can overturn. Life jackets and boat cushions will help passengers stay afloat; but it is important also that they stay with the boat. Even in the middle of a lake, it is easier for others to see a large object such as a boat, keel up, and to hear the combined shouting of several people, than it would be if all scattered and headed for shore individually. Most of the time the capsized craft will stay afloat, for there is usually a pocket of air underneath it.

Water Skiing

Local regulations in nearly every community require all water skiers to wear a flotation device, even though they might be strong swimmers. Most water skiers prefer a life-belt type device worn around the waist, for this gives the skier maximum freedom of arm movement. However, a life jacket or life vest is safer, and is recommended by the National Safety Council.

Should the skier take a tumble, there is a specific procedure to be followed by the person handling the tow boat: Slow down immediately. Turn the boat around. Move to the skier in the water *first*. The skis can be picked up later, after the swimmer is safely back in the boat.

Scuba Diving, Surfing

The word "scuba" is an abbreviation of the phrase Self-Contained Underwater Breathing Apparatus. Scuba divers wear special equipment, including fins, face mask, and oxygen tank. Only qualified experts serve as instructors, and it is suggested that young people join scuba clubs to obtain such instruction. And, even before joining the club, the boy should be thoroughly examined by a doctor, with particular emphasis on the ears, nose, and sinuses.

Most scuba instructors will not accept a beginner until they have tested the applicant themselves and are satisfied that the youngster can pass the following test:

1. Swim a minimum of 300 yards.

2. Swim a minimum of 15 yards under water.

3. Float for fifteen minutes without a flotation device.

4. Tread water for three minutes using the *feet only*.

Surfing requirements are even stricter than those for scuba diving. The United States Surfing Association has posted the following qualifications:

1. Swim a minimum of 500 yards.

2. Stay under water for a minimum of thirty seconds.

3. Control a surfboard while paddling *outward* through at least two sets of waves.

Of course, many youngsters who go surfing cannot meet these requirements. They are foolish, taking greater risk than they realize. Dad, make sure your son can pass those tests before allowing him to go surfing. It is for his own protection!

SAVING YOURSELF

On rare occasions, in spite of all safety precautions, even a good swimmer will find himself in a potentially dangerous predicament. Muscle cramps may come on suddenly, even through an inadvertent twisting of the back or legs, or an unexpected undertow may take a tiring swimmer too far out to swim back immediately.

The first rule is DON'T PANIC. A good swimmer can often overcome dangerous circumstances, provided he remains calm and remembers a few simple, basic rules of survival in the water.

Using a technique invented by Frederick Lanoue, swimming coach at Georgia Tech, which is taught to many members of our armed forces, a swimmer in distress has an excellent chance to make it safely back to shallow water, even with a muscle cramp hampering his movements. The basic idea behind Coach Lanoue's technique is to float by using a minimum of energy. In time the muscle spasm will probably ease sufficiently for the swimmer to move slowly back to shore.

The swimmer begins by using the prone float position, arms and legs dangling loosely, relaxed. To inhale, he raises his arms to the surface, lifts his head, and executes a scissors kick with his legs, pushing the water downward with the soles of his feet. He will bob to the surface momentarily, long enough to take a breath. Then he relaxes again and resumes his original prone float position, arms and legs dangling loosely.

It is possible to continue this movement for extended

periods of time, using arms and legs to thrust back to the surface.

ARTIFICIAL RESPIRATION

The most widely used, most effective means of artificial respiration in use today is the mouth-to-mouth resuscitation technique.

First, the victim is placed on his back, head tilted back so that the chin is pointing almost upward.

The victim's mouth and throat should be checked quickly, to see if any foreign matter has entered those passages. This can be done efficiently by poking a finger into the mouth of the victim, to clear out sand, mucus, or other objects which do not belong there and might obstruct breathing.

Then the rescuer places his own mouth over the victim's open mouth and blows firmly into it. For maximum effect, the blowing should be done at the average rate of twelve times per minute.

Every minute or so the rescuer should stop and check to see if any air is being exhaled by the victim.

A strong swimmer, one who uses his head and obeys the rules of safet can look forward to many hours of pleasure in the water Perhaps, someday, if the boy begins his training early enough and has the competitive urge, he may know the thrill of competition in school, in amateur athletics—or even in the Olympics itself! The swimming techniques in this book, when followed and executed faithfully, have produced champions in the past and might do the same for your son.

But, even if he never wins a medal or saves a life, the proficient young swimmer will be a stronger, more self-assured person for having attained a degree of skill in an important and pleasurable sport.

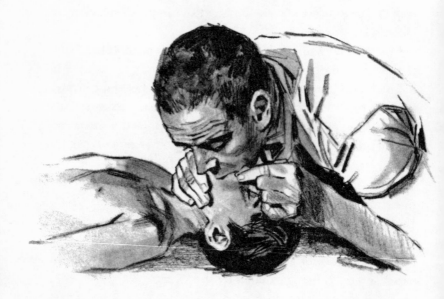

Prompt, expert application of the mouth-to-mouth resuscitation technique can mean the difference between life and death.

Index